Fernando Pessoa —
Selected English Poems

The Pessoa Edition from Shearsman Books:

Selected English Poems

Message / Mensagem
    (bilingual edition; translated by Jonathan Griffin)
    (co-publication with Menard Press)

The Collected Poems of Alberto Caeiro
    (translated by Chris Daniels)

The Collected Poems of Álvaro de Campos Vol. 1
The Collected Poems of Álvaro de Campos Vol. 2
    (translated by Chris Daniels)

Lisbon – What the Tourist Should See

Zbigniew Kotowicz: *Fernando Pessoa – Voices of a Nomadic Soul*

Fernando Pessoa

.

Selected English Poems

edited by
Tony Frazer

Shearsman Books
Exeter

First published in in the United Kingdom in 2007 by
Shearsman Books Ltd
58 Velwell Road
Exeter EX4 4LD

www.shearsman.com

ISBN-13   978-1-905700-26-4

ISBN-10   1-905700-26-1

The publisher gratefully acknowledges financial assistance from
Arts Council England.

Contents

Introduction

By now the extraordinary story of Fernando Pessoa's creative life is well-known to readers outside Portugal, thanks to a number of indefatigable translators and editors, and much scholarly work on the manuscripts – over 30,000 of them – left in the author's apartment after his death, all stored in a single large trunk.

Less well-known perhaps is that Pessoa began his poetic career writing in English, that his first publications were in English, and that he continued to write in English throughout his life, albeit on a more occasional basis once he had found his voice(s) in Portuguese. Pessoa's Portuguese *alter egos* – or heteronyms, as he termed them – have become recognised as some of the greatest writers of the 20th Century in Portuguese – not only the poets Ricardo Reis, Álvaro de Campos, Alberto Caeiro, but also the prose-writers Bernardo Soares and the Baron of Teive, with the former's *The Book of Disquiet* now widely regarded as being amongst the greatest modern prose works in the language. However, before these heteronyms were created, and indeed before the other sixty or so that have been discovered, Pessoa adopted the personae of two English poets: Charles Robert Anon, and then Alexander Search, a persona that rapidly took over from Anon and to whom some of Anon's poems were reassigned.

Pessoa was born in Lisbon in 1888, but after his father's early death, his mother remarried a military man who was Portuguese Consul in Durban, South Africa. Pessoa was then educated in South Africa until, in 1905, he returned to Lisbon where he enrolled at the University. He dropped out after less than a year of studies and thereafter made his living translating for commercial firms, from and into English and French. At the same time he developed a reputation as a poet, the major Portuguese heteronyms first appearing in 1914, and as an editor of the magazine *Orpheu*, a futurist (or 'sensationist') journal which was to have an enormous impact in its brief life – two issues were published, and a third was banned – presenting the work of several Pessoan heteronyms, as well as major new figures such as Mário de Sá-Carneiro and José de Almada Negreiros.

Pessoa would become recognised as a talented writer in his various guises – their status was not known to the wider reading public – and indeed went on to win a major prize in 1934 with his patriotic verse sequence *Mensagem* (Message), which was to be the author's only collection of poems published in Portuguese during his lifetime. Pessoa's publishing career began much earlier however, in 1918, when he self-published two chapbooks, *Antinoüs* and *35 Sonnets*. These were sent to England and the latter received some reviews, but not enough to generate the interest for which Pessoa had hoped. In 1921 Pessoa used a small inheritance to found his own small press, Olisipo, which in December of that year issued two books of the author's English poems, including 'Antinoüs', 'Inscriptions' and 'Epithalamium', a long poem dating from 1913, which had not previously been published. A large collection of Pessoa's shorter English poems, apparently written in the years 1911– 1917, *The Mad Fiddler*, has also been preserved in typescript: it was clearly intended for publication, but the reason for its remaining unpublished remains unclear, unless the closure of Olisipo after a scandal prevented it.

The selection here offers the two early long poems complete, along with the contemporaneous *Inscriptions*, and selections from *35 Sonnets* and *The Mad Fiddler*, as well as poems from later manuscripts and a small selection from the poems of Alexander Search. The Search poems are clearly juvenilia, but there is a great deal of it: 131 poems and a few fragments are presented in Luisa Freire's edition of Search's output (Lisbon: Assirio & Alvim, 1999). Pessoa grew out of this persona, just as he had grown out of C. R. Anon (who "existed" from 1904-1906), but Search is the last significant persona before the convulsion that brought forth Caeiro, Campos and Reis.

In all honesty, one cannot make great claims for Pessoa as an English poet: his diction is archaic, and many of the poems are fatally influenced by the Elizabethan and Jacobean verse that he had come across as a student in Durban. His English work remains however a fascinating prelude to the mature work, and it certainly affected his later writing in Portuguese. Pessoa remains a somewhat *foreign* poet in his native language but he and his friends – Sá-Carneiro and Negreiros – were to be the writers who modernised Portuguese poetry and set a new course for the rest of the century. The poems offered here are therefore something of a byway on the impressive road that is the work of Fernando Pessoa and his constellation of *alter egos*.

Pessoa's thinking with regard to his poetry in English may be gleaned from a few stray quotes drawn from his correspondence. In a letter of enquiry to the Poetry Society in London, dated 26 December 1912, Pessoa says with regard to contemporary Portuguese verse [the emphasis is mine. *Ed.*]:

> To give by translations an idea of contemporary Portuguese poetry, in special reference to peculiarities of style and idea, involves a difficulty precisely parallel to attempting the same thing with the *highest* English (that is, Elizabethan) style in reference to any foreign language.[1]

Then, in a letter from 24 July 1915 addressed to Alfred H. Braley, editor of *Modern Astrology*, Pessoa seeks the horoscope of Francis Bacon — who was, according to a then-fashionable theory, the real author of Shakespeare's works:

> ...[My] chief interest arises from a desire to see what in Bacon's horoscope registers his peculiar characteristic of being able to write in different styles (a fact which even non-Baconians admit) and his general faculty of transpersonalisation.

I possess . . . the characteristic to which I am alluding. I am an author, and have always found [it] impossible to write in my own personality; I have always found myself, consciously or unconsciously assuming the character of someone who does not exist, and through whose imagined agency I write. I wish to study to what this may be due by position or aspect and am therefore interested in the horoscope of the man who is known to have possessed this faculty in an extraordinary degree.[2]

In 1915 Pessoa sought publication in England, writing to the publisher John Lane, and enclosing fifteen sample poems from a proposed collection of his work, including 'Fiat Lux', although it is not clear which other poems were included. It is clear that 'Epithalamium' and 'Antinoüs' were not sent, as 'Fiat Lux' is described as being the longest of the poems in the complete manuscript and also:

I have indeed longer poems written in English, but these could not be printed in a country where there is an active public morality; so I do not think of mentioning them in this respect – that is to say, in respect of a possibility of their being published in England.[3]

This reference to morality undoubtedly alludes to the blatant sexual references in 'Epithalamium' and 'Antinoüs'.

Later that year, in an undated – and unsent – letter to Harold Monro of the Poetry Bookshop, publisher of the Imagists (and Pessoa specifically mentions his familiarity with publications by Aldington and Flint), he says of his own work:

Though in my own language, Portuguese, I am far more "advanced" than the English Imagists are, yet the English poems I send you are the nearest I have, in English, to a conventional standard of poetry.[4]

Replies have not survived, but it is clear that Pessoa's attempts to be published in London met with failure. In truth, his work was out of step with contemporary English currents, whether Georgian or Imagist, and his often exotic diction – clearly the work of someone writing in a second language – will also no doubt not have worked in his favour. Pessoa actually intended to send his own translation of one of his Portuguese poems ('Chuva Obliqua' or 'Slanting Rain'), as a further sample of his work, but it would appear that this translation was never made, fascinating though it would have been to have it. There are however some translations by Pessoa of poems assigned to the Álvaro de Campos heteronym, which have been included in the critical edition of the Campos poems published by Imprensa Nacional – Casa da Moeda in Lisbon.

Pessoa's almost-juvenilia in English is worth reading as background to his poetry in Portuguese – to which four companion volumes in this series are being devoted. Such is the fascination that Pessoa exerts, some seventy years after his death, that each scrap from his trunk is poured over, and these English scraps are worth more than a cursory glance: they are an introduction to one of the oddest and most compelling voices in international literary modernism. We anglophones cannot claim him for ourselves, but we have a small part of him, and that is no bad thing.

Tony Frazer
Exeter, 2007

Notes:
[1] Fernando Pessoa *Correspondência 1905-1922* (ed. Manuela Parreira da Silva. Lisbon: Assirio & Alvim, 1999): p. 60.
[2] ibid, p. 169.
[3] ibid, p, 175.
[4] ibid, p. 193.

from

English Poems I-III:

from *35 Sonnets*
Epithalamium
Antinoüs
Inscriptions

IV

I could not think of thee as piecèd rot,
Yet such thou wert, for thou hadst been long dead;
Yet thou liv'dst entire in my seeing thought
And what thou wert in me had never fled.
Nay, I had fixed the moments of thy beauty –
Thy ebbing smile, thy kiss's readiness,
And memory had taught my heart the duty
To know thee ever at that deathlessness.
But when I came where thou wert laid, and saw
The natural flowers ignoring thee sans blame,
And the encroaching grass, with casual flaw,
Framing the stone to age where was thy name,
    I knew not how to feel, nor what to be
    Towards thy fate's material secrecy.

VII

Thy words are torture to me, that scarce grieve thee –
That entire death shall null my entire thought;
And I feel torture, not that I believe thee,
But that I cannot disbelieve thee not.
Shall that of me that now contains the stars
Be by the very contained stars survived?
Thus were Fate all unjust. Yet what truth bars
An all unjust Fate's truth from being believed?
Conjecture cannot fit to the seen world
A garment of her thought untorn or covering,
Or with her stuffed garb forge an otherworld
Without herself its dead deceit discovering;
    So, since all may be, an idle thought well may
    Less idle thoughts, self-known no truer, dismay.

X

As to a child, I talked my heart asleep
With empty promise of the coming day,
And it slept rather for my words made sleep
Than from a thought of what their sense did say.
For did it care for sense, would it not wake
And question closer to the morrow's pleasure?
Would it not edge nearer my words, to take
The promise in the meting of its measure?
So, if it slept, 'twas that it cared but for
The present sleepy use of promised joy,
Thanking the fruit but for the forecome flower
Which the less active senses best enjoy.
    Thus with deceit do I detain the heart
    Of which deceit's self knows itself a part.

XI

Like to a ship that storms urge on its course,
By its own trials our soul is surer made.
The very things that make the voyage worse
Do make it better; its peril is its aid.
And, as the storm drives from the storm, our heart
Within the peril disimperilled grows;
A port is near the more from port we part –
The port whereto our driven direction goes.
If we reap knowledge to cross-profit, this
From storms we learn, when the storm's height doth drive –
That the black presence of its violence is
The pushing promise of near far blue skies.
    Learn we but how to have the pilot-skill,
    And the storm's very might shall mate our will.

XIII

When I should be asleep to mine own voice
In telling thee how much thy love's my dream,
I find me listening to myself, the noise
Of my words othered in my hearing them.
Yet wonder not: this is the poet's soul.
I could not tell thee well of how I love,
Loved I not less by knowing it, were all
My self my love and no thought love to prove.
What consciousness makes more by consciousness,
It makes less, for it makes it less itself.
My sense of love could not my love rich-dress
Did it not for it spend love's own love-pelf.
    Poet's love's this (as in these works I prove thee):
    I love my love for thee more than I love thee.

XIV

We are born at nightfall and we die ere morn,
And the whole darkness of the world we know,
How can we guess its truth, to darkness born,
The obscure consequence of absent glow?
Only the stars do teach us light. We grasp
Their scattered smallnesses with thoughts that stray,
And, though their eyes look through night's complete mask,
Yet they speak not the features of the day.
Why should these small denials of the whole
More than the black whole the pleased eyes attract?
Why what it calls "worth" does the captive soul
Add to the small and from the large detract?
    So, out of light's love wishing it night's stretch,
    A nightly thought of day we darkly reach.

XV

Like a bad suitor desperate and trembling
From the mixed sense of being not loved and loving,
Who with feared longing half would know, dissembling
With what he'd wish proved what he fears soon proving,
I look with inner eyes afraid to look,
Yet perplexed into looking, at the worth
This verse may have and wonder, of my book,
To what thoughts shall't in alien hearts give birth.
But, as he who doth love, and, loving, hopes,
Yet, hoping, fears, fears to put proof to proof,
And in his mind for possible proofs gropes,
Delaying the true proof, lest the real thing scoff,
 I daily live, i'th' fame I dream to see,
 But by my thought of others' thought of me.

XVII

My love, and not I, is the egoist.
My love for thee loves itself more than thee;
Ay, more than me, in whom it doth exist,
And makes me live that it may feed on me.
In the country of bridges the bridge is
More real than the shores it doth unsever;
So in our world, all of Relation, this
Is true – that truer is Love than either lover.
This thought therefore comes lightly to Doubt's door –
If we, seeing substance of this world, are not
Mere intervals, God's Absence and no more,
Hollows in real Consciousness and Thought.
 And if 'tis possible to Thought to bear this fruit,
 Why should it not be possible to Truth?

XXIV

Something in me was born before the stars
And saw the sun begin from far away.
Our yellow, local day on its wont jars,
For it hath communed with an absolute day.
Through my Thought's night, as a worn robe's heard trail
That I have never seen, I drag this past
That saw the Possible like a dawn grow pale
On the lost night before it, mute and vast.
It dates remoter than God's birth can reach,
That had no birth but the world's coming after.
So the world's to me as, after whispered speech,
The cause-ignored sudden echoing of laughter.
    That 't has a meaning my conjecture knows,
    But that 't has meaning's all its meaning shows.

XXVI

The world is woven all of dream and error
And but one sureness in our truth may lie –
That when we hold to aught our thinking's mirror
We know it not by knowing it thereby.
For but one side of things the mirror knows,
And knows it colded from its solidness.
A double lie its truth is; what it shows
By true show's false and nowhere by true place.
Thought clouds our life's day-sense with strangeness, yet
Never from strangeness more than that it's strange
Doth buy our perplexed thinking, for we get
But the words' sense from words – knowledge, truth, change.
 We know the world is false, not what is true.
 Yet we think on, knowing we ne'er shall know.

Epithalamium

I

Set ope all shutters, that the day come in
Like a sea or a din!
Let not a nook of useless shade compel
Thoughts of the night, or tell
The mind's comparing that some things are sad,
For this day all are glad!
'Tis morn, 'tis open morn, the full sun is
Risen from out the abyss
Where last night lay beyond the unseen rim
Of the horizon dim.
Now is the bride awaking. Lo! she starts
To feel the day is home
Whose too-near night will put two different hearts
To beat as near as flesh can let them come.
Guess how she joys in her feared going, nor opes
Her eyes for fear of fearing at her joy.
Now is the pained arrival of all hopes.
With the half-thought she scarce knows how to toy.
Oh, let her wait a moment or a day
And prepare for the fray
For which her thoughts not ever quite prepare!
With the real day's arrival she's half wroth.
Though she wish what she wants, she yet doth stay
Her dreams yet mergèd are
In the slow verge of sleep, which idly doth
The accurate hope of things remotely mar.

II

Part from the windows the small curtains set
Sight more than light to omit!
Look on the general fields, how bright they lie
Under the broad blue sky,
Cloudless, and the beginning of the heat
Does the sight half ill-treat!
The bride hath wakened. Lo! she feels her shaking
Heart better all her waking!
Her breasts are with fear's coldness inward clutched
And more felt on her grown,
That will by hands other than hers be touched
And will find lips sucking their budded crown.
Lo! the thought of the bridegroom's hands already
Feels her about where even her hands are shy,
And her thoughts shrink till they become unready.
She gathers up her body and still doth lie.
She vaguely lets her eyes feel opening.
In a fringed mist each thing
Looms, and the present day is truly clear
But to her sense of fear.
Like a hue, light lies on her lidded sight,
And she half hates the inevitable light.

III

Open the windows and the doors all wide
Lest aught of night abide,
Or, like a ship's trail in the sea, survive
What made it there to live!
She lies in bed half waiting that her wish

Grow bolder or more rich
To make her rise, or poorer, to oust fear,
And she rise as a common day were here.
That she would be a bride in bed with man
The parts where she is woman do insist
And send up messages that shame doth ban
From being dreamed but in a shapeless mist.
She opes her eyes, the ceiling sees above
Shutting the small alcove,
And thinks, till she must shut her eyes again,
Another ceiling she this night will know,
Another house, another bed, she lain
In a way she half guesses; so
She shuts her eyes to see not the room she
Soon will no longer see.

IV

Let the wide light come through the whole house now
Like a herald with brow
Garlanded round with roses and those leaves
That love for its love weaves!
Between her and the ceiling this day's ending
A man's weight will be bending.
Lo! with the thought her legs she twines, well knowing
A hand will part them then;
Fearing that entering in her, that allowing
That will make softness begin rude at pain.
If ye, glad sunbeams, are inhabitèd
By sprites or gnomes that dally with the day,
Whisper her, if she shrink that she'll be bled,
That love's large bower is doored in this small way.

V

Now will her grave of untorn maidenhood
Be dug in her small blood.
Assemble ye at that glad funeral
And weave her scarlet pall,
O pinings for the flesh of man that often
Did her secret hours soften
And take her willing and unwilling hand
Where pleasure starteth up.
Come forth, ye moted gnomes, unruly band,
That come so quick ye spill your brimming cup;
Ye that make youth young and flesh nice
And the glad spring and summer sun arise;
Ye by whose secret presence the trees grow
Green, and the flowers bud, and birds sing free,
When with the fury of a trembling glow
The bull climbs on the heifer mightily!

VI

Sing at her window, ye heard early wings
In whose song joy's self sings!
Buzz in her room along her loss of sleep,
O small flies, tumble and creep
Along the counterpane and on her fingers
In mating pairs. She lingers.
Along her joined-left legs a prophecy
Creeps like an inward hand.
Look how she tarries! Tell her: fear not glee!
Come up! Awake! Dress for undressing! Stand!
Look how the sun is altogether all!

Life hums around her senses petalled close.
Come up! Come up! Pleasure must thee befall!
Joy to be plucked, O yet ungathered rose!

VII

Now is she risen. Look how she looks down,
After her slow down-slid night-gown,
On her unspotted white of nakedness
Save where the beast's difference from her white frame
Hairily triangling black below doth shame
Her to-day's sight of it, till the caress
Of the chemise cover her body. Dress!
Stop not, sitting upon the bed's hard edge,
Stop not to wonder at by-and-bye, nor guess!
List to the rapid birds i'th' window ledge!
Up, up and washed! Lo! she is up half-gowned,
For she lacks hands to have power to button fit
The white symbolic wearing, and she's found
By her maids thus, that come to perfect it.

VIII

Look how over her seeing-them-not her maids
Smile at each other their same thought of her!
Already is she deflowered in others' thoughts.
With curious carefulness in inlocked braids,
With hands that in the sun minutely stir,
One works her hair into concerted knots.
Another buttons tight the gown; her hand,
Touching the body's warmth of life, doth band

Her thoughts with the rude bridegroom's hand to be.
The first then, on the veil placed mistily,
Lays on her head, her own head sideways leaning,
The garland soon to have no meaning.
The other, at her knees, makes the white shoon
Fit close the trembling feet, and her eyes see
The stockinged leg, road upwards to that boon
Where all this day centres its revelry.

IX

Now is she gowned completely, her face won
To a flush. Look how the sun
Shines hot and how the creeper, loosed, doth strain
To hit the heated pane!
She is all white, all she's awaiting him.
Her eyes are bright and dim.
Her hands are cold, her lips are dry, her heart
Pants like a pursued hart.

X

Now is she issued. List how all speech pines
Then bursts into a wave of speech again!
Now is she issued out to where the guests
Look on her daring not to look at them.
The hot sun outside shines.
A sweaty oiliness of hot life rests
On the day's face this hour.
A mad joy's pent in each warm thing's hushed power.

XI

Hang with festoons and wreaths and coronals
The corridors and halls!
Be there all round the sound of gay bells ringing!
Let there be echoing singing!
Pour out like a libation all your joy!
Shout, even ye children, little maid and boy
Whose belly yet unfurred yet whitely decks
A sexless thing of sex!
Shout out as if ye knew what joy this is
You clap at in such bliss!

XII

This is the month and this the day.
Ye must not stay.
Sally ye out and in warm clusters move
To where beyond the trees the belfry's height
Does in the blue wide heaven a message prove,
Somewhat calm, of delight.
Now flushed and whispering loud sally ye out
To church! The sun pours on the ordered rout,
And all their following eyes clasp round the bride:
They feel like hands her bosom and her side;
Like the inside of the vestment next her skin,
They round her round and fold each crevice in;
They lift her skirts up, as to tease or woo
The cleft hid thing below;
And this they think at her peeps in their ways
And in their glances plays.

XIII

No more, no more of church or feast, for these
Are outward to the day, like the green trees
That flank the road to church and the same road
Back from the church, under a higher sun trod.
These have no more part than a floor or wall
In the great day's true ceremonial.
The guests themselves, no less than they that wed,
Hold these as nought but corridors to bed.
So are all things, that between this and dark
Will be passed, a dim work
Of minutes, hours seen in a sleep, and dreamed
Untimed and wrongly deemed.
The bridal and the walk back and the feast
Are all for each a mist
Where he sees others through a blurred hot notion
Of drunk and veined emotion,
And a red race runs through his seeing and hearing,
A great carouse of dreams seen each on each,
Till their importunate careering
A stopped, half-hurting point of mad joy reach.

XIV

The bridegroom aches for the end of this and lusts
To know those paps in sucking gusts,
To put his first hand on that belly's hair
And feel for the lipped lair,
The fortress made but to be taken, for which
He feels the battering ram grow large and itch.
The trembling glad bride feels all the day hot

On that still cloistered spot
Where only her nightly maiden hand did feign
A pleasure's empty gain.
And, of the others, most will whisper at this,
Knowing the spurt it is;
And children yet, that watch with looking eyes,
Will now thrill to be wise
In flesh, and with big men and women act
The liquid tickling fact
For whose taste they'll in secret corners try
They scarce know what still dry.

XV

Even ye, now old, that to this come as to
Your past, your own joy throw
Into the cup, and with the younger drink
That which now makes you think
Of what love was when love was. (For not now
Your winter thoughts allow).
Drink with the hot day, the bride's sad joy and
The bridegroom's haste inreined,
The memory of that day when ye were young
And, with great paeans sung
Along the surface of the depths of you,
You paired and the night saw
The day come in and you did still pant close,
And still the half-fallen flesh distending rose.

XVI

No matter now or past or future. Be
Lover's age in your glee!
Give all your thoughts to this great muscled day
That like a courser tears
The bit of Time, to make night come and say
The maiden mount now her first rider bears!
Flesh pinched, flesh bit, flesh sucked, flesh girt around,
Flesh crushed and ground,
These things inflame your thoughts and make ye dim
In what ye say or seem!
Rage out in naked glances till ye fright
Your ague of delight,
In glances seeming clothes and thoughts to hate
That fleshes separate!
Stretch out your limbs to the warm day outside,
To feel it while it bide!
For the strong sun, the hot ground, the green grass,
Each far lake's dazzling glass,
And each one's flushed thought of the night to be
Are all one joy-hot unity.

XVII

In a red bacchic surge of thoughts that beat
On the mad temples like an ire's amaze,
In a fury that hurts the eyes, and yet
Doth make all things clear with a blur around,
The whole group's soul like a glad drunkard sways
And bounds up from the ground!
Ay, though all these be common people heaping

To church, from church, the bridal keeping,
Yet all the satyrs and big pagan haunches
That in taut flesh delight and teats and paunches,
And whose course, trailing through the foliage, nears
The crouched nymph that half fears,
In invisible rush, behind, before
This decent group move and with hot thoughts store
The passive souls round which their mesh they wind,
The while their rout, loud stumbling as if blind,
Makes the hilled earth wake echoing from her sleep
To the lust in their leap.

XVIII

Io! Io! There runs a juice of pleasure's rage
Through these frames' mesh,
That now do really ache to strip and wage
Upon each others' flesh
The war that fills the womb and puts milk in
The teats a man did win,
The battle fought with rage to join and fit
And not to hurt or hit!
Io! Io! Be drunken like the day and hour!
Shout, laugh and overpower
With clamour your own thoughts, lest they a breath
Utter of age or death!
Now is all absolute youth, and the small pains
That thrill the fillèd veins
Themselves are edged in a great tickling joy
That halts ever ere it cloy.
Put out of mind all things save flesh and giving
The male milk that makes living!

Rake out great peals of joy like grass from ground
In your o'ergrown soul found!
Make your great rut dispersedly rejoice
With laugh or voice,
As if all earth, hot sky and tremulous air
A mighty cymbal were!

XIX

Set the great Flemish hour aflame!
Your senses of all leisure maim!
Cast down with blows that joy even where they hurt
The hands that mock to avert!
All things pick up to bed that lead ye to
Be naked that ye woo!
Tear up, pluck up, like earth who treasure seek,
When the chest's ring doth peep,
The thoughts that cover thoughts of the acts of heat
This great day does intreat!
Now seem all hands pressing the paps as if
They meant them juice to give!
Now seem all things pairing on one another,
Hard flesh soft flesh to smother,
And hairy legs and buttocks balled to split
White legs mid which they shift.
Yet these mixed mere thoughts in each mind but speak
The day's push love to wreak,
The man's ache to have felt possession,
The woman's man to have on,
The abstract surge of life clearly to reach
The bodies' concrete beach.
Yet some work of this doth the real day don.

Now are skirts lifted in the servant's hall,
And the whored belly's stall
Ope to the horse that enters in a rush,
Half late, too near the gush.
And even now doth an elder guest enmesh
A flushed young girl in a dark nook apart,
And leads her slow to move his produced flesh.
Look how she likes with something in her heart
To feel her hand work the protruded dart!

XX

But these are thoughts or promises or but
Half the purpose of rut,
And this is lust thought-of or futureless
Or used but lust to ease.
Do ye the circle true of love pretend,
And, what Nature, intend!
Do ye actually ache
The horse of lust by reins of life to bend
And pair in love for love's creating sake!
Bellow! Roar! Stallions be or bulls that fret
On their seed's hole to get!
Surge for that carnal complement that will
Your flesh's young juice thrill
To the wet mortised joints at which you meet
The coming life to greet,
In the tilled womb that will bulge till it do
The plenteous curve of spheric earth renew!

XXI

And ye, that wed to-day, guess these instincts
Of the concerted group in hints
Yourselves from Nature naturally have,
And your good future brave!
Close lips, nude arms, felt breasts and organ mighty,
Do your joy's night work rightly!
Teach them these things, O day of pomp of heat!
Leave them in thoughts such as must make the feat
Of flesh inevitable and natural as
Pissing when wish doth press!
Let them cling, kiss and fit
Together with natural wit,
And let the night, coming, teach them that use
For youth is in abuse!
Let them repeat the link, and pour and pour
Their pleasure till they can no more!
Ay, let the night watch over their repeated
Coupling in darkness, till thought's self, o'erheated,
Do fret and trouble, and sleep come on hurt frames,
And, mouthing each one's names,
They in each other's arms dream still of love
And something of it prove!
And, if they wake, teach them to recommence,
For an hour was far hence;
Till their contacted flesh, in heat o'erblent
With joy, sleep sick, while, spent
The stars, the sky pale in the East and shiver
Where light the night doth sever,
And with clamour of joy and life's young din
The warm new day come in.

Lisbon, 1913

Antinoüs

The rain outside was cold in Hadrian's soul.

The boy lay dead
On the low couch, on whose denuded whole,
To Hadrian's eyes, whose sorrow was a dread,
The shadowy light of Death's eclipse was shed.

The boy lay dead, and the day seemed a night
Outside. The rain fell like a sick affright
Of Nature at her work in killing him.
Memory of what he was gave no delight,
Delight at what he was was dead and dim.

O hands that once had clasped Hadrian's warm hands,
Whose cold now found them cold!
O hair bound erstwhile with the pressing bands!
O eyes half-diffidently bold!
O bare female male-body such
As a god's likeness to humanity!
O lips whose opening redness erst could touch
Lust's seats with a live art's variety!
O fingers skilled in things not to be told!
O tongue which, counter-tongued, made the blood bold!
O complete regency of lust throned on
Raged consciousness's spilled suspension!
These things are things that now must be no more.
The rain is silent, and the Emperor
Sinks by the couch. His grief is like a rage,
For the gods take away the life they give
And spoil the beauty they made live.
He weeps and knows that every future age
Is looking on him out of the to-be;
His love is on a universal stage;
A thousand unborn eyes weep with his misery.

Antinoüs is dead, is dead for ever,
Is dead for ever and all loves lament.
Venus herself, that was Adonis' lover,
Seeing him, that newly lived, now dead again,
Lends her old grief's renewal to be blent
With Hadrian's pain.

Now is Apollo sad because the stealer
Of his white body is for ever cold.
No careful kisses on that nippled point
Covering his heart-beats' silent place restore
His life again to ope his eyes and feel her
Presence along his veins Love's fortress hold.
No warmth of his another's warmth demands.
Now will his hands behind his head no more
Linked, in that posture giving all but hands,
On the projected body hands implore.

The rain falls, and he lies like one who hath
Forgotten all the gestures of his love
And lies awake waiting their hot return.
But all his arts and toys are now with Death.
This human ice no way of heat can move;
These ashes of a fire no name can burn.

O Hadrian, what will now thy cold life be?
What boots it to be lord of men and might?
His absence o'er thy visible empery
Comes like a night,
Nor is there morn in hopes of new delight.
Now are thy nights widowed of love and kisses;
Now are thy days robbed of the night's awaiting;
Now have thy lips no purpose for thy blisses,

Left but to speak the name that Death is mating
With solitude and sorrow and affright.

Thy vague hands grope, as if they had dropped joy.
To hear that the rain ceases lift thy head,
And thy raised glance take to the lovely boy.
Naked he lies upon that memoried bed;
By thine own hand he lies uncoverèd.
There was he wont thy dangling sense to cloy,
And uncloy with more cloying, and annoy
With newer uncloying till thy senses bled.

His hand and mouth knew games to reinstal
Desire that thy worn spine was hurt to follow.
Sometimes it seemed to thee that all was hollow
In sense in each new straining of sucked lust.
Then still new turns of toying would he call
To thy nerves' flesh, and thou wouldst tremble and fall
Back on thy cushions with thy mind's sense hushed.

"Beautiful was my love, yet melancholy.
He had that art, that makes love captive wholly,
Of being slowly sad among lust's rages.
Now the Nile gave him up, the eternal Nile.
Under his wet locks Death's blue paleness wages
Now war upon our wishing with sad smile."

Even as he thinks, the lust that is no more
Than a memory of lust revives and takes
His senses by the hand, his felt flesh wakes,
And all becomes again what 'twas before.
The dead body on the bed starts up and lives
And comes to lie with him, close, closer, and

A creeping love-wise and invisible hand
At every body-entrance to his lust
Whispers caresses which flit off yet just
Remain enough to bleed his last nerve's strand,
O sweet and cruel Parthian fugitives!

So he half rises looking on his lover,
That now can love nothing but what none know.
Vaguely, half-seeing what he doth behold,
He runs his cold lips all the body over.
And so ice-senseless are his lips that, lo!,
He scarce tastes death from the dead body's cold,
But it seems both are dead or living both
And love is still the presence and the mover.
Then his lips cease on the other lips' cold sloth.

Ah, there the wanting breath reminds his lips
That from beyond the gods hath moved a mist
Between him and this boy. His finger-tips,
Still idly searching o'er the body, list
For some flesh-response to their waking mood.
But their love-question is not understood:
The god is dead whose cult was to be kissed!

He lifts his hand up to where heaven should be
And cries on the mute gods to know his pain.
Let your calm faces turn aside to his plea,
O granting powers! He will yield up his reign.
In the still deserts he will parchèd live,
In the far barbarous roads beggar or slave,
But to his arms again the warm boy give!
Forego that space ye meant to be his grave!

Take all the female loveliness of earth
And in one mound of death its remnant spill!
But, by sweet Ganymede, that Jove found worth
And above Hebe did elect to fill
His cup at his high feasting, and instil
The friendlier love that fills the other's dearth,
The clod of female embraces resolve
To dust, O father of the gods, but spare
This boy and his white body and golden hair!
Maybe thy better Ganymede thou feel'st
That he should be, and out of jealous care
From Hadrian's arms to thine his beauty steal'st.

He was a kitten playing with lust, playing
With his own and with Hadrian's, sometimes one
And sometimes two, now linking, now undone;
Now leaving lust, now lust's high lusts delaying;
Now eyeing lust not wide, but from askance
Jumping round on lust's half-unexpectance;
Now softly gripping, then with fury holding,
Now playfully playing, now seriously, now lying
By th' side of lust looking at it, now spying
Which way to take lust in his lust's withholding.

Thus did the hours slide from their tangled hands
And from their mixèd limbs the moments slip.
Now were his arms dead leaves, now iron bands;
Now were his lips cups, now things that sip;
Now were his eyes too closed and now too looking;
Now were his uncontinuings frenzy working;
Now were his arts a feather and now a whip.

That love they lived as a religion
Offered to gods that come themselves to men.
Sometimes he was adorned or made to don
Half-vestures, then in statued nudity
Did imitate some god that seems to be
By marble's accurate virtue men's again.
Now was he Venus, white out of the seas;
And now was he Apollo, young and golden;
Now as Jove sate he in mock judgment over
The presence at his feet of his slaved lover;
Now was he an acted rite, by one beholden,
In ever-repositioned mysteries.

Now he is something anyone can be.
O stark negation of the thing it is!
O golden-haired moon-cold loveliness!
Too cold! too cold! and love as cold as he!
Love through the memories of his love doth roam
As through a labyrinth, in sad madness glad,
And now calls on his name and bids him come,
And now is smiling at his imaged coming
That is i'th' heart like faces in the gloaming –
Mere shining shadows of the forms they had.

The rain again like a vague pain arose
And put the sense of wetness in the air.
Suddenly did the Emperor suppose
He saw this room and all in it from far.
He saw the couch, the boy, and his own frame
Cast down against the couch, and he became
A clearer presence to himself, and said
These words unuttered, save to his soul's dread:

"I shall build thee a statue that will be
To the continued future evidence
Of my love and thy beauty and the sense
That beauty giveth of divinity.
Though death with subtle uncovering hands remove
The apparel of life and empire from our love,
Yet its nude statue, that thou dost inspirit,
All future times, whether they will't or not,
Shall, like a gift a forcing god hath brought,
Inevitably inherit.

"Ay, this thy statue shall I build, and set
Upon the pinnacle of being thine, that Time
By its subtle dim crime
Will fear to eat it from life, or to fret
With war's or envy's rage from bulk and stone.
Fate cannot be that! Gods themselves, that make
Things change, Fate's own hand, that doth overtake
The gods themselves with darkness, will draw back
From marring thus thy statue and my boon,
Leaving the wide world hollow with thy lack.

"This picture of our love will bridge the ages.
It will loom white out of the past and be
Eternal, like a Roman victory,
In every heart the future will give rages
Of not being our love's contemporary.

"Yet oh that this were needed not, and thou
Wert the red flower perfuming my life,
The garland on the brows of my delight,
The living flame on altars of my soul!
Would all this were a thing thou mightest now

Smile at from under thy death-mocking lids
And wonder that I should so put a strife
Twixt me and gods for thy lost presence bright;
Were there nought in this but my empty dole
And thy awakening smile half to condole
With what my dreaming pain to hope forbids."

Thus went he, like a lover who is waiting,
From place to place in his dim doubting mind.
Now was his hope a great intention fating
Its wish to being, now felt he he was blind
In some point of his seen wish undefined.

When love meets death we know not what to feel.
When death foils love we know not what to know.
Now did his doubt hope, now did his hope doubt;
Now what his wish dreamed the dreams sense did flout
And to a sullen emptiness congeal.
Then again the gods fanned love's darkening glow.

"Thy death has given me a higher lust –
A flesh-lust raging for eternity.
On mine imperial fate I set my trust
That the high gods, that made me emperor be,
Will not annul from a more real life
My wish that thou should'st live for e'er and stand
A fleshly presence on their better land,
More lovely yet not lovelier, for there
No things impossible our wishes mar
Nor pain our hearts with change and time and strife.

"Love, love, my love! thou art already a god.
This thought of mine, which I a wish believe,

Is no wish, but a sight, to me allowed
By the great gods, that love love and can give
To mortal hearts, under the shape of wishes –
Of wishes having undiscovered reaches –,
A vision of the real things beyond
Our life-imprisoned life, our sense-bound sense.
Ay, what I wish thee to be thou art now
Already. Already on Olympic ground
Thou walkest and art perfect, yet art thou,
For thou needst no excess of thee to don
Perfect to be, being perfection.

"My heart is singing like a morning bird.
A great hope from the gods comes down to me
And bids my heart to subtler sense be stirred
And think not that strange evil of thee
That to think thee mortal would be.

"My love, my love, my god-love! Let me kiss
On thy cold lips thy hot lips now immortal,
Greeting thee at Death's portal's happiness,
For to the gods Death's portal is Life's portal.

"Were no Olympus yet for thee, my love
Would make thee one, where thou sole god mightst prove,
And I thy sole adorer, glad to be
Thy sole adorer through infinity.
That were a universe divine enough
For love and me and what to me thou art.
To have thee is a thing made of god's stuff
And to look on thee eternity's best part.

"But this is true and mine own art: the god
Thou art now is a body made by me,
For, if thou art now flesh reality
Beyond where men age and night cometh still,
'Tis to my love's great making power thou owest
That life thou on thy memory bestowest
And mak'st it carnal. Had my love not held
An empire of my mighty legioned will,
Thou to gods' consort hadst not been compelled.

"My love that found thee, when it found thee did
But find its own true body and exact look.
Therefore when now thy memory I bid
Become a god where gods are, I but move
To death's high column's top the shape it took
And set it there for vision of all love.

"O love, my love, put up with my strong will
Of loving to Olympus, be thou there
The latest god, whose honey-coloured hair
Takes divine eyes! As thou wert on earth, still
In heaven bodifully be and roam,
A prisoner of that happiness of home,
With elder gods, while I on earth to make
A statue for thy deathlessness' seen sake.

"Yet thy true deathless statue I shall build
Will be no stone thing, but that same regret
By which our love's eternity is willed.
One side of that is thou, as gods see thee
Now, and the other, here, thy memory.
My sorrow will make that men's god, and set
Thy naked memory on the parapet

That looks upon the seas of future times.
Some will say all our love was but our crimes;
Others against our names the knives will whet
Of their glad hate of beauty's beauty, and make
Our names a base of heap whereon to rake
The names of all our brothers with quick scorn.
Yet will our presence, like eternal Morn,
Ever return at Beauty's hour, and shine
Out to the East of Love, in light to enshrine
New gods to come, the lacking world to adorn.

"All that thou art now is thyself and I.
Our dual presence has its unity
In that perfection of body which my love,
By loving it, became, and did from life
Raise into godness, calm above the strife
Of times, and changing passions far above.

"But since men see more with the eyes than soul,
Still I in stone shall utter this great dole;
Still, eager that men hunger by thy presence,
I shall to marble carry this regret
That in my heart like a great star is set.
Thus, even in stone, our love shall stand so great
In thy statue of us, like a god's fate,
Our love's incarnate and discarnate essence,
That, like a trumpet reaching over seas
And going from continent to continent,
Our love shall speak its joy and woe, death-blent,
Over infinities and eternities.

"And here, memory or statue, we shall stand,
Still the same one, as we were hand in hand

Nor felt each other's hand for feeling feeling.
Men still will see me when thy sense they take.
The entire gods might pass, in the vast wheeling
Of the globed ages. If but for thy sake,
That, being theirs, hadst gone with their gone band,
They would return, as they had slept to wake.

"Then the end of days when Jove were born again
And Ganymede again pour at his feast
Would see our dual soul from death released
And recreated unto joy, fear, pain –
All that love doth contain;
Life – all the beauty that doth make a lust
Of love's own true love, at the spell amazed;
And, if our very memory wore to dust,
By some god's race of the end of ages must
Our dual unity again be raised."

It rained still. But slow-treading night came in,
Closing the weary eyelids of each sense.
The very consciousness of self and soul
Grew, like a landscape through dim raining, dim.
The Emperor lay still, so still that now
He half forgot where now he lay, or whence
The sorrow that was still salt on his lips.
All had been something very far, a scroll
Rolled up. The things he felt were like the rim
That haloes round the moon when the night weeps.

His head was bowed into his arms, and they
On the low couch, foreign to his sense, lay.
His closed eyes seemed open to him, and seeing
The naked floor, dark, cold, sad and unmeaning.

His hurting breath was all his sense could know.
Out of the falling darkness the wind rose
And fell; a voice swooned in the courts below;
And the Emperor slept.

                              The gods came now
And bore something away, no sense knows how,
On unseen arms of power and repose.

Lisbon, 1915.

Inscriptions

I

We pass and dream. Earth smiles. Virtue is rare.
Age, duty, gods weigh on our conscious bliss.
Hope for the best and for the worst prepare.
The sum of purposed wisdom speaks in this.

II

Me, Chloe, a maid, the mighty fates have given,
Who was nought to them, to the peopled shades.
Thus the gods will. My years were but twice seven.
I am forgotten in my distant glades.

III

From my villa on the hill I long looked down
Upon the muttering town;
Then one day drew (life sight-sick, dull hope shed)
My toga o'er my head
(The simplest gesture being the greatest thing)
Like a raised wing.

IV

Not Cecrops kept my bees. My olives bore
Oil like the sun. My several herd lowed far.
The breathing traveller rested by my door.
The wet earth smells still; dead my nostrils are.

V

I conquered. Far barbarians hear my name.
Men were dice in my game,
But to my throw myself did lesser come:
I threw dice, Fate the sum.

VI

Some were as loved loved, some as prizes prized.
A natural wife to the fed man my mate,
I was sufficient to whom I sufficed.
I moved, slept, bore and aged without a fate.

VII

I put by pleasure like an alien bowl.
Stern, separate, mine, I looked towards where gods seem.
From behind me the common shadow stole.
Dreaming that I slept not, I slept my dream.

VIII

Scarce five years passed ere I passed too.
Death came and took the child he found.
No god spared, or fate smiled at, so
Small hands, clutching so little round.

IX

There is a silence where the town was old.
Grass grows where not a memory lies below.
We that dined loud are sand. The tale is told.
The far hoofs hush. The inn's last light doth go.

X

We, that both lie here, loved. This denies us.
My lost hand crumbles where her breasts' lack is.
Love's known, each lover is anonymous.
We both felt fair. Kiss, for that was our kiss.

XI

I for my city's want fought far and fell.
I could not tell
What she did want, that knew she wanted me.
Her walls be free,
Her speech keep such as I spoke, and men die,
That she die not, as I.

XII

Life lived us, not we life. We, as bees sip,
Looked, talked and had. Trees grow as we did last.
We loved the gods but as we see a ship.
Never aware of being aware, we passed.

XIII

The work is done. The hammer is laid down.
The artisans, that built the slow-grown town,
Have been succeeded by those who still built.
All this is something lack-of-something screening.
The thought whole has no meaning
But lies by Time's wall like a pitcher spilt.

XIV

This covers me, that erst had the blue sky.
This soil treads me, that once I trod. My hand
Put these inscriptions here, half knowing why;
Last, and hence seeing all, of the passing band.

from

The Mad Fiddler

Spell

From the moonlit brink of dreams
    I stretch foiled hands to thee,
O borne down other streams
    Than eye can think to see!
O crowned with spirit-beams!
    O veiled spiritually!

My dreams and thoughts abate
    Their pennons at thy feet,
O angel born too late
    For fallen man to meet!
In what new sensual state
    Could our twined lives feel sweet?

What new emotion must
    I dream to think thee mine?
What purity of lust?
    O tendrilled as a vine
Around my caressed trust!
    O dream-pressed spirit-wine!

undated

The Shining Pool

Go: thou hast nothing to forgive.
To dream is better than to live.

But he shall see the rising sun
Who leaveth everything undone;
Whose mind from his attention's task
Strays like the shifting of a mask.

He only shall through greener vales
    Than even those that shine right through
The window-panes of children's tales
    Wander, who thinks the world anew.

Only for him who sits and sings
    On the stiles and forgets his road
Does the fairies' bird spread her wings
    And the fairies' flowers grow more broad.

He shall not find a hand to feed
The silent sources of his need.
No one shall point the rill where he
May slake the thirst of infancy.

But greener valleys than To-Day
And dearer thoughts than Far Away
Shall tap at his window and wake
His freshness other thirsts to slake.

So, like a seamstress sitting still
    At a window in the sunset
    Of a village no steps have met,
He shall belong to nothing ill,

But incorporeal, like a wish,
　　His soul shall like a rainbow cross
　　The rain-green pastures of his loss
And earth shall blossom into speech.

1.ii.1915

Looking at the Tagus

She led her flocks beyond the hills,
   Her voice backs to me in the wind,
And a thirst for her sorrow fills
   All that in me is undefined.

Spiritual lakes walled round with crags
   Sleep in the hollows of her song.
There her unbathing nudeness lags
   And looks on its pooled shadow long.

But what is real in all this is
   Only my soul, the eve, the quay
And, shadow of my dream of this,
   An ache for a new ache in me.

But what is she that sorrow is?
   And what is she that sorrow lacks?
What last thing of love is this bliss
   That follows in her missèd tracks?

The lilies lie between hearts and hands.
   Life is too little for the moon.
Yet let the left trees slightly stir
   And hope wakes for she will come soon.

undated

If I could carve my poems in wood

If I could carve my poems in wood,
By children they would be understood,

So near to the sense things have in God
Are both my poems and children's thought.

For a child knows that logic and meaning
Are only nothing nothing screening,

And a child is one divinely aware
That all things are toys and all things are fair.

That a thimble, a stone and a cotton-reel
Are things we can quite divinely feel,

And that, if we make men out of those things,
They are really men, not imaginings.

I would therefore I could take my verse
Out of mere ideas and better it worse

To visible carving or drawing or what
My verses could be resembling that.

Then would I be the children's poet.
And, though perhaps I might never know it

With the outer sense that makes life sadder,
In every innocent face made gladder

God would be giving my soul the sense,
Lost back of knowledge, of recompense –

The sense of children more children still
When, acting my poems at their glad will,

They, playing with toys, with legs incurled,
Lightly err the visible world.

17.ix.1916

Prayer

Our Lady of Useless Tears,
　　Thine is my heart's best shrine.
I am sick with the gorging years,
　　I am drunk with the bitter wine
Of having but cares and fears,
　　Of knowing but how to pine.

It is useless to pray to thee,
　　But my heart is full of pain.
Thy glance would be charity,
　　Even if the look were disdain.
Give me that I may be
　　A child like thine again.

My sense of me is all tears.
　　I pity my heart too much.
Oh, a cradle for my fears
　　And the hem of thy garment to clutch!
Oh, wert thou alive and near us,
　　And thy hand a hand that could touch!

I do not know how to pray.
　　My heart is a torn pall.
See how my hair grows gray.
　　Oh, teach my lips to call
On thy name night and day
　　As if that name were all.

My fathers' faith doth rise
　　To my lips this sick hour.
I pray to thee with mine eyes
　　Rosaries of anguish. Oh dower

My soul with at least sweet lies
   Of thy suffering son's power!

I have forgotten the taste
   Of faith, and ache for prayer.
My heart is a garden laid waste.
   Oh, thy hand on my hair
Like a mother's hand let rest
   And let me die with it there!

1913?

Rivers

Many rivers run
    Down to many seas.
All my cares are one:
    On what river of these
    Could my heart have peace?

Two banks to each river.
    None where I may stray
Hearing the rushes shiver
    And seeing the river ever
    Pass, yet seem to stay.

Maybe there is another
    River, but far in Me.
There I may meet the Brother
    Of my eternity.
    In what God will this be?

Nothing: all the leaves
    Fallen from the tree.
Many a river cleaves
    Its way past what grieves
    To what grieves in me.

28.ii.1913-1.iii.1913

The Broken Window

My heart is silent as a look.
    There is a home beyond the hills.
My heart is silent as a look.
    My home is there, beyond the hills.

I bear my heart like an old curse.
    There is no reason for regret.
I bear my heart like an old curse.
    Why should we reason or regret?

My heart dwells in me like a ghost.
    Beyond the hills my hope lies dead.
My heart dwells in me like a ghost.
    Beyond my hope the hills lie dead.

They took away my heart like weeds.
    It was not true that I should live.
They took away my heart like weeds.
    I could not think it true to live.

Now there are great stains in my heart.
    They are like blood-stains on a floor.
Now there are great stains in my heart.
    And my heart lies upon the floor.

The room is closed for ever now.
    My heart is now buried alive.
My heart is closed for ever now.
    The whole room is buried alive.

1915?

Fiat Lux

Into a vision before me the world
Flowered, and it was as when a flag, unfurled,
Suddenly shows unknown colours and signs.
    Into an unknown meaning, evident
And unknown ever, it outspread its lines
    Of meaning to my passive wonderment.
The outward and the inward became one.
Feelings and thoughts were visible in shapes,
And flowers and trees as feelings, thoughts. Great capes
Stood out of Soul, thrust into conscious seas,
And on all this a man-sky spoke its breeze.

Each thing was linked into each other thing
By links of being past imagining,
But visible, as if the skeleton
Were visible and the flesh round it, each one
As if a separate thing visibly alone.

There was no difference between a tree
And an idea. Seeing a river be
And the exterior river were one thing.
The bird's soul and the motion of its wing
Were an inextricable oneness made.
And all this I saw, seeing not, dismayed
With the New God this vision told me of;
For this was aught I could not speak nor love,
But a new sentiment not like all others,
Nought like the human feelings, men are brothers
In feeling, woke on my astonished spirit.
With a great suddenness did this disinherit
That thought that looks through mine eyes of the pelf
Of ordered seeing that maketh it itself.

O horror set with mad joy to appal!
O self-transcendency of all!
O inner infinity of each thing, that now
Suddenly was made visible and local, though
No manner of speech to speak these things in words
Followed that vision! Sight whose sense absurds
Likeness of like, and makes disparity
Contiguous innerly to unity!

How to express what, seen, is not expressed
To the struck sight that sees it? How to know
What comes to senses' threshold to bestow
A visible ignorance upon the knowing?
How to obey the analogy-behest,
Community in unity to prove
The intellectual meaning of to love,
Shipwrecking difference upon the sight
Renewed from God to Inwards infinite?

Nothing: the exterior world inner expressed,
The flower of the whole vision of the world
        Into its colour of absolutely meaning
In the night unfurled,
And therefore nought unfurling, abstract, that,
        Vision self-screening,
Patent invisible fact.

Nothing: all,
And I centre of to recall,
        As if Seeing were a god.
The rest the presence of to see,
Hollow self-sensed infinity,

And all my being-not-souled-to-oneness trod
To fragments in my sight-dishevelled sight.

This Night is Light.

15.ii.1916

Uncollected Poems

1901-1917

Separated from thee, treasure of my heart

Separated from thee, treasure of my heart,
By earth despised, from sympathy free,
Yet winds may quaver and hearts may waver,
I'll never forget thee.

Soft seem the chimes of boyhood sweet
To one who is no more free,
But let winds quaver and men's hearts waver,
I'll never forget thee.

In a dim vision, from school hailing
Myself a boyish form, I see,
And winds have quavered and men's hearts wavered,
But I've not forgotten thee.

Since first thy form divine I saw,
While from school I came with glee,
Winds have quavered and men's heart's wavered,
But I've not forgotten thee.

Since a simple boyish passion
I entertained for thee,
Though winds have quavered and men's hearts wavered,
I've not forgotten thee.

The stars shine bright, the moon looks love,
From over the moonlit sea,
Winds have quavered and men's hearts wavered
And thou hast forgotten me.

Separated from thee, treasure of my heart,
By earth despised, from sympathy free,
Yet winds may quaver and hearts may waver,
    But I'll never forget thee.

12.i.1901

Now there are no Janus' temple-doors . . .

Now are no Janus' temple-doors thrown wide
To utter thoughts of war upon the land.
Now doth no double facing God divide
Him from himself, that sight of him may brand
The symbol of opposed things upon
Our hearts that at our eyes on him are thrown.
Now do no pagan hearts tremble at Mars' name
Because ill-auguring birds like clouds have flown
O'er nations' frontiers, nor do oracles frame
Strange answers unto ears of armoured chiefs,
Replies that leave perplexed their perplexed eyes
That know not whether that heart-pang they hear
Is the first grief heralding their peoples' griefs
Or the strange cold that the Gods' mysteries
Speak to his soul that is to conquest near.

No. All is dead that wreathed war round with Gods.
Nor omens mute, nor the foiled sacrifice,
No strange words spoken by spilt blood on sods.
Nay, nor the sicker sense that vice and sloth,
When in a people's heart they nestle both
Do on them call the wrath of heaven, us move.
Our souls are void, like a stage mummer's cries
And our hate and our love mock hate and love.

Something of coldness, like the coming winter,
Crosses our autumn like a profecy.
Round our leaves now no swallows circle and twitter.
No more, no more, shall we heart-wholesome be.
There is a sadness that with us doth stay
Like a billetted guest, and far away
Our ultimate death awaits us like a sea.

Alas! that even the poesy of wars
Should, like a tired thing, have gone where things go.
Alas! alas! that we have come thus far
Knowing still the same nothing that we know,
To meet more than ourselves, nor no throe
That shall be herald of a newer man.
And ever as the old woes the cold new woe
Fills with its deathless measure our life's span.

No, even the Christian manner of love or hate
Is dead. No God that lives in us survives
The winter in us that snow-kills God and Fate
And has iced o'er the rivers of our lives.
With cuirass and with pike we laid aside
All that made battle worth the death in it.
Our science-made war-gestures now deride
The great eternal things that war doth fit
With helm and armour.
With mortal pomp yet pomp. We are on death's side.

All is as if were not part of it.
All clashes, rings and turmoils as if far.
The foiled imagining within our wit
Ousts war's clear image with bare thought of war.
Our plans are cold, our courage cold, our eyes
When they look inwards dream but the far plain
And vague, picture-seen faces and their pain
Touches no sense of ours, nor do dreamed cries
Rise in us. What cold thing has become of
Our very hatred? What way has strength gone?
We die as if the sky were not above
Our heads and beneath us sand, grass and stone.

The great eternal presence of all things
No longer doth with us collaborate
To lift our hearts up on invisible wings
And bid us tremble at the thrill of Fate.
The possible fall of empires doth no more
Touch us with that great and mysterious dread
That John on Pathmos saw rise o'er his head
Like a space-filling sea without a shore.

Alas! our nobler fear has gone away
Where our weariness pointed. We are blind
And learned to blindness. Our wild gestures stray
From us like leaves that fall far off with the wind,
And we fight clearly, coldly, night and day.

These things I thought, knowing that far behind
My visible horizon war was slave
Of that Invisible Master who doth wave
His speechless hand o'er continents and seas
And men like reaped things fall, and the blind wind
With groping hands that in the night are blind
Touches the dead men's faces' mysteries.

This I thought when, lo! before me there was
A door of iron, or what iron seemed,
An unsized portal, and its live-seeming lock
Seemed all the uses of a lock to mock.
To see that door was to know none could pass
Through it, nor could its other-side be dreamed.

A ribbon of broad stairs led up to it
But had no meaning, like a laugh unseen,
I looked and the door seemed to sway as hit

By blows, but no blows fell on it. That screen
Was interposed between me and no scene,
Yet, like an eye staring from out the night,
It touched my heart cold with its iron mean.
And this was not in space nor in a light.

Somewhere in me where dreams do themselves show
And have an inner meaning God doth know,
The door was set, and it seemed to my soul
That there since some inner eternity
It ever had been and I something had seen,
Yet half forgot, that like a half-shown scroll,
Concealed its sense in what it showed to me.

And lo! as my heart looked, the door grew clear
As a near-lit thing seen in a black night,
And a great sense of a great coming fear
Was fear already in my heart's affright.
Then as I looked I saw – yet it did seem
That in my vision that had ever been –
From beneath the strange door down the steps flow
A string of silent blood, that step by step,
Fell with a motion desolate and slow.

The thin red stream seemed conscious of its course
Though its course seemed to be none, but to fall.
I looked and it fell ever, with a force
Of relinquishment to its fall, a knell
To some hope in me, and the blood
That ever was but a small line did flood
All my pained soul and made it red. The spell
Of its thin redness spread o'er my thought's mood
And all my thoughts became a great red wall
Set up in front of what in me doth brood.

Then everything shifted, yet was the same.
I looked on as one who sees a child's game
And finds its eyes at interest in it
And knows not why. A sense of end did hit
My power of having feelings with a rain
That did with deep red all my dim soul stain
As it had stained that soul.

Then all the outer world was dashed to night
And, though no floor remained, no sides, no light
To that space-missed new world, set far from being,
Yet by some clearer virtue of my seeing
All I saw was without nor left nor right
With a name to it, without a place
Even in itself, without an I to see.
The mere great door and the red blood's thin trace
And all the rest was void and mystery.

Then all again seemed changing unto some
New, unimaginable and fearful thing.
The door and that blood-line seemed to come
A strange unfeatured Face looking out through
The Universe's whole frame, traversing
It like light an invisible glass – a wing
Belonging to no bird our thoughts construe.

Then the door seemed to recede – nay, to have
Receded, when I knew not, nor was there
A when, for Time seem'd as seems a far wave
On a wide sea, something gone past. The bare
Eternal door seemed to have gone to the end
Of a visible infinity, and all
That now remained on which my soul could spend
Its terror was the blood ever at its fall.

Then, though still the same small line of red,
The blood seemed to grow glass and in it I saw
A mighty river full of strange things – dead
Men, children, wrecks of bridges, cities, thrones,
And still the line was a small red line, (...)
Of other meaning than that
That before God for the clear world atones.

But the (...) visions in that line contained
Seemed wide as space. The red line seemed a slit
In a thin door through which our eyes can see
Large fields, a city and the whole sky stained
With clouds, and all this in the line could be;
And from some unknown where I looked on it.

It seemed the edge of a cube opening
Sideways to sides of visions, more and more.
Now and then across its glass – like being a wing
Passed a tremor ran over everything
That had in it a clear and tragic being.
Then ceased. And from, past space, the door
Still held my unconscious consciousness of seeing.

It seemed sometimes a bright, red moving veil
And through it as through a stained window I guessed
A night and stars on a vague pale day pressed,
On a same horizon desolate and pale.

Then, as I stared, suddenly before me,
Like a fan suddenly opened, the blood-line
Took space from side to side, leaving naught to me
Left or right of it. Its red (...) fact
Became a red Niagara, a cataract.

But there were no steps, nothing: it did fall
As if drawn in the air, over no edge, and all
Was this and this was its own mystery.

Then lo! over the edge, no longer now,
But empires rolled, and I saw Greece and Rome
Pass. And still over the eternal flow
Reddened from left to right my inner sight's home
Of seeing. And all like to God's blood did come
Like a great rain off a huge thorn-crowned brow.

And I saw more and more strange empires roll
Down and some I knew not, nor seeing them, guessed.
Awhile their falling the fall's brink caressed
Then they sunk down somewhere within my soul,
And my soul was the soul of all the world,
And from my (...) eyes that saw all this
Suddenly I felt, as if a flag unfurled,
God in me look out at these mysteries.

My eyes seemed windows of another sight
Of someone set behind my soul in the night
Looking through my eyes and my sight, mine own
Was but a glass those unknown eyes looked through,
And still the vision was blood falling down
In cataracts into Mystery, red and slow.

I became one with world and Fate and God,
And the great River that came on and fell
Let me see through its veil of (...) blood
The stars shine and a vague moonlight, then fell
Something from me. The cataract came more near
To my sight; then it seemed into mine eyes

To creep to become with them and the fear
To pass behind them into some soul (...).

Then all that did remain was the stars' light
And again in the dark infinity
My pity and my dread alone with me
And my dream's meaning like a paling night.

17.i.1915

Second Sight

Whene'er thou dost undo
Thy dark, strange hair before the wind
And the wind takes it up and makes it woo
Tumult and violence in the way it sweeps
Along the air, mingling, unmingling, undefined
In the snake-like madness it keeps,

Then I do know
That somewhere whence dreams come
And passions go,
Somewhere in that world contrary to this,
Yet landscaped, peopled as this is,
In a great southern sea
There is a storm and a hurled wreck
On rising rocks that cannot reck
For human misery.

The two things are but one.
Thy floating hair is that great ship undone
In a tossed, turbulent, dashed ocean.
Neither precedeth nor doth cause the other
Nor are the two as brother and brother,
But absolutely one, samely the same,
They have somehow an equal name
Where speech is of the essence of what is.

A real sight, like God's, should see the kiss
Of the wind through thy hair and the far storm
One thing, – yet two things because we see two
When we conceive them one, the double form
Coming to oneness in what we construe.

Therefore I grieve when thou letst thy hair take
The wind upon its long, thin, changing fingers,
For that sight of me that translates that to
The sterner meaning in what world I know
Only through what in me is not here awake, –
That sight of that mad wreck visibly lingers
And does in my imagination ache.

Alas! all things are linked, and we know not
Half the contents of our each casual thought.
We never see save one little dreamed bit
Of each feeling we have; we pass through it
Like rapid travellers that scarce can see
What they pass by and what they see see erringly.

What is the meaning of my writing this?
Nothing, save that this is,
I know not why, something I know and must
Utter, the purpose of it being with
That secret Being that made my body of dust
Bear my soul's ignored presence, and that breath
Of life that survives my each moment's death.

4.xi.1915

Desolation

Here where the rugged hills
Their gnarled loose bases grip into the earth,
And nothing save the sorrow of our birth
From seeing the seeing spirit fills,
Here where, among the grim, deserted stones,
No hope of green for desertness atones,
Or water's sound
Make sweet the solitude around,
Here may I lay
This day
My head
Upon the ground and say
No better bed
Can he who has but himself for life have,
Nor better grave.

The sterile part
Of love, feeling, was given me.
From the humanness even of a broken heart
God set me free.
Out of my destiny no flower was made
To grow.
All in me fated was not even to fade
Or e'en a vain and transient glory show.

The very need
For love or joy or the human part of thought,
Pride, and the abstract greed
For truth, that lifts the heart and doth allot
A value of self and world to consciousness –
Even this bliss
My empty heart has not.

O weary born,
Faded begun,
Gone from unseen shores to seen shores forlorn,
Sent out of sun-gone unto unborn sun!
The singer of his wish
To sing no song,
The poor spendthrift rich
With knowing not for what to long.

The Hyperion dispossessed
Ere birth
Of that sun-mansion set out beyond rest
Above the wide-lit stretches of the earth.

The uncrowned king
That never saw the land
Of which he oft doth sing,
And whose lost path he cannot understand
Nor know how to dream steps him there to bring.

The priest deferred
From the inner shrine.
The thought but never uttered word,
The fore-spilt wine,
The anxiousness for hope, the cold divine
Of anguish that no anguish human is,
The solitary pine
On the lone hill of consciousness.

The hour
The lord
Returns
Back to the polluted bower,

Home to the intransitable ford,
Again to the ice-padlocked burns.

The shadow
Fixedly thrown
On the green meadow
By a tree overgrown
With leaves, but fruitless, flowerless and lone.

The last
Sight of a shore
Which the unhalting ship doth pass
And where it never shall pass more;
But where the heart-dim sailor knows
Homes are happy because not his,
Lips warm because never his lips to kiss,
Gardens fair because therein grows
The unfound rose,
Hours soft, fate fresh, life a real fairy elf
Because somewhere outside himself

16.x.1916

Salute to the Sun's Entry into Aries

Now at the doorway of the coming year,
Ye nymphs do gather and the garlands twine
That heroes' sons will bear
Fifty years hence in their remembering hands
And of their fathers speak with shining eyes
And of the war that stained the lands.
Weave ye the garlands, for the fame will pass,
And their grandchildren of grandchildren will
No more remember, neither care
Who their ancestor was
Who did that old crown, now scarce a crown, hear
For all must pass, that Time may have his fill.

Weave ye the garlands therefore, for this hour
Will not survive beyond the memory
Of those yet near to it who have the power
The hour somewhat like what it was to see.
Weave ye the garlands, weave
That their memory may live
Awhile, and if that mean that fame is nought,
Weave still the garlands with a gentle thought,
For weaving them, know ye
What to Time's elder shades you yet may give.
The days are heavy with the blood of men,
The year reels like a shattered wall
When the wind comes out of the caves of night.
 Our minds are equal with the shaking ...
We know not on what power to call
Or which side of the Truth lies right.

Alas! alas! all sides are right in war,
And that impartial vision born of peace,
And that the Gods alone can have,

Lives only in our wish that dim wars mar,
Breathes only in the halls of our release
From all the human things for which we crave.
But these are thoughts, and life is grief and fear.
Weave ye the garlands, lest the coming year
Forget, like ye, the fallen to remember
And the victors to greet.
Weave ye the garlands made
Of some strange flower that lasts unto December
And lay them at Fate's unseen feet.

Ay, for not for the heroes nor the slain
Weave ye the garlands woven with your pain.
Not for the fallen do your cheeks awhile
Flush then grow pale and your proud pain smile.
Not for a man nor for a nation do
Your garlands outreach Time
Perhaps and in eternal regions chime
With the sense of their fame who were e'er true.

For Fate alone all garlands woven are.
Unto Fate's feet the rivers of our tears
Perennial run, nor is there aught more far
Alas! than mere Fate that outwits the sun,
And that in circles round its empty name
Carries the vain course of our sterile fame
And great men as great nations equal lead
Vainly around the frame
Of nothing, like a wind along a mead.

Yet, whether for some man or for no man,
Whether for personal hopes or Fate no one,
Your garlands weave, lest the year come and span

With days fame-empty the task e'er begun.
Weave garlands, green glad garlands, garlands sad,
Garlands of all sorts, if they glory mean,
Carry your woven garlands to their grave ...
The rest is something that cannot be had –
The void as of a ship sunk nor more seen
Beneath the wave.

9.iii.1917

Selected Later Poems

I have outwatched the Lesser Wain

I have outwatched the Lesser Wain, and seen
The remnant stars grow pale; but the used night
Has to the thought that used it sterile been,
Nor lost that use by pressure of delight.

My fixed, impatient thought no reason read;
What I scarce read my unthought thought made stray;
My soul between the living and the dead
Was a blown vapour, without place or way.

What the morn brought or took I cannot tell,
That had no use to bring or use to find.
All night I lay under the barren spell.
The day cannot dispel what the void wind

Ruinous built in the shorn night: its glow
Can but the night's made desert brightly show.

18.i.1924

Arethusa

Still Arethusa keeps her course,
For, though the corporal dark of earth
Stifle, like an unconscious nurse,
The impulse for her second birth,
Yet her true will must ever be
These captive waves that shall be free.

So the forgotten water ever
With withdrawn life and hid emotion
Moves on in darkness, still a river,
Towards a sun upon an ocean;
And the found place there will not cease
To be the river's, not the sea's.

So keeps she, under the void dark
Of her oppressed seclusion still
Her careful self whose soul shall work
Towards the outlet from the hill,
Past hived vaults and humid walls
And the dropped noise of waterfalls.

Uncaught throughout the spell of caves,
Forlorn under the mother stone,
Still the great destined river craves
Its purpose, liquid and alone,
And more, yet less, under the hills
Its unresisting motion wills.

So ever, while time frets the rocks
And space shuts dark the godless flow,
She runs, a will in waves that flocks
Around a darkness for a glow;

And onward still, because it is
What shall be, and the Gods are this.

And, still remembering to forget,
Still onward because Fate inclines,
Veiled Arethusa still doth wet
With purpose the weird cavern shrines,
Where, past their blind, dead, solid being,
Her watery will moves on to seeing.

Dim under phosphorescent zones
Of darkness wronged and stalactites,
Or complete darkness, where the moans
Of waters wail for destined sights,
Her course, that knows no day, doth still
Work out to day its nightly will,

Till, bright at last in the aired arms
Of the lone rocks laid in the sea,
Bare Arethusa free her charms
To light and to its panic glee,
And the sea clasp her, as she were
Venus there born and mistress there.

6.xi.1930

The Master said you must not heed

The Master said you must not heed
What others talk of at their need.

Under the happy trees they sit
That talk of nothing and of wit.
Under the silent trees they stand
That talk of mirth and no man's land.
Under the sulky trees they lie
That wonder of the earth and sky.

This was the matter of the song
No one could sing or well or long.
This was the substance of the tale
No one could tell unless it fail.
This was the subject of the verse
The last one made, lest earth be worse.

So the collateral nightingale
Forgot its music and its tale.
So the lark rose and found but air
And false dominion everywhere.
So the dropt eagle, losing prey,
Swept by and owned but the void day.

Yet what the secret of all this
May be or was none now can guess.
Perhaps beyond what thought defines,
Like wine drawn from sleep-smothered vines,
There lies some chance that someone may
Make shade and sleep of yesterday.

But whether this be sense or nought,
Surely it was a careful thought

To have the lawn so nicely laid
Out and the critics all gainsaid.
It was the reason and the home.
The rest is why 'tis right to roam.

2.ii.1933

A low, sad wind fills the lone night

A low, sad wind fills the lone night
With its one solitary sound.
I have forgotten what delight
Delight has. In the vague around
All sleep is consecrated ground.

Alas for all I ever hoped!
The sheep crop what it lies beneath.
Its grave is where the mountain sloped
When mountains were, but now the heath
Is all the life above its death.

Moan, solitary wind that wakes
When the day sleeps! Moan vague and low!
That which I never was now slakes
Its thirst where reeds cluster round lakes
Of silence, or mute rivers go.

To-morrow shall be yesterday
Lest life forget what it is ever.
I shall myself cast this away
That I am now, and myself sever
From what of me weeps by this river.

This river of the haunted night
That under stars I do not see
Has neither purpose nor delight,
Moan, solitary wind, and be
This life's unchanging, shoreless sea!

13.iii.1933

I love this world and all these men because

I love this world and all these men because
I shall not love them long. That we do die
I believe not, bound fast to higher laws,
But that we lose this world do not deny.

This light that in the sea makes many a light,
This breeze so soft when least we feel it most,
May be replaced by a diviner sight
Or by a truer breeze; but these are lost.

Like some strange trick of childhood that was ill
Yet had the child, already I regret
From some grand future world sublime and still,
The childhood that I never shall forget –

No, nor these toys of sense – this world, these men –,
Dear now when had because dear when lost then.

8.x.1933

Selected Poems of Alexander Search

1904-1907

On Death

When I consider how each day's career
Doth with its footstep swift yet heavy tread
Approach my soul to those great regions dread
And bring my youth to timeless death more near,

Though strange and sad to me it doth appear
That I (who now feel life) must soon be dead,
Some vague, uncertain sorrow weighs my head
And whelms my coward mind with lengthless fear,

Nevertheless though sorrow rage and tear
My heart, yet I each moment's boon shall seize.
And shape rude laughter from each heart-felt moan:

Not without hope is most extreme despair,
I know not death and think it no release –
The bad indeed is better than the unknown.

May 1904

Sonnet

Could I say what I think, could I express
My every hidden and too-silent thought,
And bring my feelings, in perfection wrought,
To one unforced point of living stress;

Could I breathe forth my soul, could I confess
The inmost secrets to my nature brought;
I might be great, yet none to me hath taught
A language well to figure my distress.

Yet day and night to me new whispers bring,
And night and day from me old whispers take ...
Oh for a word, one phrase in which to fling

All that I think and feel, and so to wake
The world; but I am dumb and cannot sing,
Dumb as yon clouds before the thunders break.

1904

Mania of Doubt

All things unto me are queries
That from normalness depart,
And their ceaseless asking wearies
        My heart.
Things are and seem, and nothing bears
The secret of the life it wears.

All things' presence e'er is asking
Questions of disturbing pain
With dreadful hesitation tasking
        My brain.
How false is truth? How much doth seem
Since dreams are all and all's a dream.

Before mystery my will faileth
Torn with war within the mind,
And Reason like a coward quaileth
        To find
More than themselves all things reveal
Yet that they with themselves conceal.

19.vi.1907

Justice

There was a land, which I suppose,
Where everyone had a crooked nose;

And the crooked nose that everyone had
In no manner did make him sad.

But in that land a man was born
Whose nose more straight and clean was worn;

And the men of that land with a public hate
Killed the man whose nose was straight.

28.vii.1907

Epitaph

Here lies who thought himself the best
Of poets in the world's extent;
In life he had nor joy nor rest.

He filled with madness many a song,
And at whatever age he died
Thus many days he lived too long.

He lived in powerless egotism,
His soul tumultuous and disordered
By thought and feeling's endless schism.

In everything he had a foe
And without courage bore his part
In life's interminable woe.

He was a slave to grief and fear
And incoherent thoughts he had
And wishes unto madness near.

Those whom he loved, by arts of ill
He treated worse than foes; but he
His own worst enemy was still.

He of himself ever did sing,
Incapable of modesty,
Lock'd in his wild imagining.

Useless was all his toilless trouble
Empty of sense his fears and pains
And many of them were ignoble.

Vile thus and worthless his distress;
His words, though bitterer far than hate,
His bitter soul could not express.

Thus was he miserable and bad,
Who yet could sob in tenderness –
And none was found to know him mad.

Let not a healthy mind pollute
His grave, but fitly there will pass
The traitor and the prostitute;

The drunkard and the wencher there
May pass, but quick, lest they should ponder,
Perchance, that pleasure is but air.

Each weak and execrable mind
Which plagued man with its rottenness
Its conscious master here will find,

Conscious, for in him he could tell
Madness and ill were what they were,
But neither did he will to quell.

Pass by therefore ye who can weep;
Let rottenness work in neglect,
While the rough winds the dead leaves sweep.

His slumbering brother to the sod
Not even in imagining
Disturb not with the name of God.

But let him lie at peace for ever
Far from the eyes and mouths of men
And from what him from them did sever.

He was a thing that God had wrought
And to the sin of having lived
He joined the crime of having thought.

The Story of Solomon Waste

This is *all* the story of Solomon Waste.

Always hurrying yet never in haste,
He fussed and worked and toiled all frothing
And at the end of all did nothing.
This is *all* the story of Solomon Waste.

He lived in wishing and in striving,
And nothing came of all his living;
He worked and toiled in pain and sweat,
And nothing came out of all that.
This is *all* the story of Solomon Waste.

He thought much and had no conviction,
His feeling was at best affliction;
Though tender he and hating evil
He might have gained the name of devil.
His every wish and resolution
Even in his mind was but confusion.
This is *all* the story of Solomon Waste.

And things begun and never ended,
And much undone and much intended,
And all things wrong yet never mended:
This is *all* the story of Solomon Waste.

Each day new projects did betray,
Yet each day was like every day.
He was born and died and between these
He worried himself himself to tease.
He bustled, worried, moved and cried
But in his life no more's descried

Than two clear facts: he lived and died.
This is *all* the story of Solomon Waste.

11.viii. 1907

Publishing History

35 Sonnets

First published as a chapbook – *35 Sonnets,* Lisbon: Monteiro & Co., 1918. They have been republished many times since the author's death, with the major recent versions being in *Poemas Ingleses, Tomo I,* ed. João Dionisio. Lisbon: Imprensa Nacional – Casa da Moeda, 1993, and *Poesia Inglesa I,* ed. Luísa Freire, Lisbon: Assíro & Alvim, 2000 (henceforward, Freire 1).

Epithalamium

First published in *English Poems III*; Lisbon: Olisipo, 1921. Recent republications are in Dionisio, *op. cit.,* and Freire 1.

Antinoüs

First published in *Antinoüs. A Poem by Fernando Pessoa*; Lisbon: Monteiro & Co., 1918, and subsequently reprinted in the author's *English Poems I–II,* Lisbon: Olisipo, 1921. Recent republications are in Dionisio, *op. cit.,* and Freire 1.

Inscriptions

First published in *English Poems I–II,* Lisbon: Olisipo, 1921. Recent republications are in Dionisio, *op. cit.,* and Freire 1.

The Mad Fiddler

Manuscript unpublished in book form during the author's lifetime. The individual poems presented here have all been collected in Freire 1, as well as in *Poemas Inglesas, Tomo III, The Mad Fiddler,* ed. Marcus Angioni & Fernando Gomes. Lisbon: Imprensa Nacional – Casa da Moeda, 1999. The following poem was published during the author's lifetime:
'Spell', in *Contemporanea,* Vol. III / 9, Lisbon, May 1923.

Uncollected Poems (1901-1917)

All published in *Poesia Inglesa II,* ed. Luísa Freire, Lisbon: Assíro & Alvim, 2000 (henceforward, Freire 2). First publications listed below.
'Separated from thee, treasure of my heart'
   Fernando Pessoa, *Obra Poética,* 2nd Edn., ed. Maria Aliete Galhoz. Rio de Janeiro: Aguilar Ed., 1965; Jorge de Sena (ed) *Poemas Ingleses de Fernando Pessoa,* Lisbon, Ática, 1974.

'Now are no Janus' temple-doors thrown wide'
First published in G.R. Lind, 'Poesias Inglesas Inéditas de
Fernando Pessoa sobre a Primeira Guerra Mundial', in *Oci-
dente*, Lisbon, N° 405. January 1972, pp. 24-29.

'Second Sight'
First publication: G.R. Lind, 'Oito Poemas Ingleses Inédi-
tos de Fernando Pessoa', in *Ocidente*, Lisbon, N° 362, Vol.
LXXIV, June 1968.

'Desolation'
First publication: G.R. Lind, in *Poetica*, Vol 2, N° 2, Munich,
April 1966.

'Salute to the Sun's Entry into Aries'
First publication: G.R. Lind, 'Poesias Inglesas Inéditas de
Fernando Pessoa sobre a Primeira Guerra Mundial', *ed.cit.*

Selected Later Poems
All published in Freire 2. Previous publications listed below.
'I have outwatched the Lesser Wain'; 'Arethusa'; 'The Master
said you must not heed'
Previously published in *Poesia Inglesa*, ed. Luisa Freire. Rio
de Janeiro: Livros Horizonte, 1995.

'A low, sad wind fills the lone night'
First published in H.D. Jennings, *Os dois Exílios. Fernando
Pessoa na África do Sul*, Porto, Centro de Estudos Pessoanos,
1984.

'I love this world and all these men because'
First published in Teresa Rita Lopez (ed), *Pessoa Inédito*,
Lisbon, Livros Horizonte, 1993.

Selected Poems of Alexander Search
All published in Alexander Search, *Poesia*, ed. Luísa Freire, Assírio
& Alvim, Lisbon, 1999. First publications listed below.
'On Death'
First published by Eduardo Lourenço in 'Considerações
sobre o Proto-Pessoa. Do tempo da Morte à Morte do tempo'
in *Actas do 1° Congreso Internacional de Estudos Pessoanos*,
Porto, Brasilia Ed. — Centro de Estudos Pessoanos, 1979.

Sonnet: 'Could I say what I think'; 'Mania of Doubt'; 'Justice'
All first published by G R Lind in 'Die Englische Jugend-

dichtung Fernando Pessoas' in *Aufsätze zur Portugiesischen Kulturgeschichte*, Band 6, Münster, 1966.

'Epitaph'; 'The Story of Solomon Waste'
First published by G R Lind, 'A Poesia Juvenil de Fernando Pessoa', *Humboldt*, Hamburg, Vol. 8, N° 17, 1968.

Printed in the United Kingdom by
Lightning Source UK Ltd., Milton Keynes
140829UK00001B/27/A